Sir Robert Hunter
Co-founder and 'Inventor' of the National Trust

Foreword

O f the triumvirate of founders of the National Trust, Sir Robert Hunter was the least conspicuous but the most effective. He was its architect and engineer, its steady hand on the helm. He was also the Trust's first Chairman. Of Hunter it could be said, they also serve who get on and do the work. Without him, there might one day have been a national trust, but not the National Trust.

Above:
Sir Robert
Hunter at work.

Hunter was by profession a lawyer, his official post being Solicitor to the Post Office. But he was a legal polymath. An enthusiasm for building preservation, town planning and the open air led him into concert with Octavia Hill and the firebrand Lake District champion, Canon Hardwicke Rawnsley. He brought to their campaigning a legal mind and an understanding that all the campaigning in the world was nothing without a solid base in law and proper organization. He had worked for many years for the Commons Preservation Society and was the first of the trust's founders to use the phrase 'National Trust' during discussions over its foundation. Hunter campaigned for the protection of ancient monuments and wrote the Trust's own Act of Parliament in 1907. He was also Chairman of Hampstead Garden Suburb.

On Hunter's death in November 1913, the committee recorded its grief at the 'sense of irreparable loss' and its indebtedness to his 'unwearying industry, his great business capacity, his unrivalled knowledge of the law'. It is to Hunter that we owe what is still part of the Trust's character today, that of a national conservation movement, statutorily embedded and charged with holding land inalienably on behalf of the nation. He worked tirelessly for this cause, and the Trust today is his monument.

Simon Jenkins
Chairman, National Trust

Sir Robert Hunter, 1844–1913
by Ben Cowell

Sir Robert Hunter is one of three figures now regarded as the principal founders of the National Trust. The other two were the social housing reformer Octavia Hill and the campaigner for the Lake District Canon Hardwicke Rawnsley. Of the three Hunter is perhaps the least well known or remembered today, yet this is in many ways a travesty of history.

Numerous people were involved in setting up the National Trust for Places of Historic Interest and Natural Beauty, to give its full title, but it simply would not have happened without Hunter's contribution. Indeed, since he came up with the idea for the organization (and quite possibly its name), paved the way for its legal creation and served as its first Chairman, a claim could be made for Hunter as the man who 'invented' the National Trust.

Such a claim by no means diminishes the contribution of the others involved. After all, Hunter's legal expertise and political connections were the perfect complement to Hill's social concerns and Rawnsley's campaigning energy.

In reasserting Hunter's role in making the National Trust happen and in his leading it in its early years, we must ask why have the achievements of this devoted, hard-working and unassuming man been so easily downplayed? Perhaps it is because of those very qualities that endeared him to his family, friends and colleagues: his dedication to public duty, his intense concentration and application, and his modest, self-effacing manner.

Hunter was never one to crave public attention in pursuit of his objectives, preferring instead to win arguments through the power of his meticulous reasoning and evidence. Nevertheless he was astute in cultivating and maintaining political networks and was a highly influential figure behind the scenes of the late-Victorian movement for landscape and building preservation in Britain.

Hunter's love of nature, of open spaces, and of the infinite pleasures to be had from countryside never deserted him throughout his life. Rawnsley described him as having a fierce fighting spirit, a cheery optimism, and 'an almost child's power of simple enjoyment'. His career took off with his work for the Commons Preservation Society, using his legal training to prevent the enclosure of open landscapes including Hampstead Heath and Epping Forest.

He was promoted to become the most senior lawyer at the General Post Office, where

Below: **The three principal founders of the National Trust (left to right): Robert Hunter (1844–1913); Octavia Hill (1838–1912); Canon Hardwicke Rawnsley (1851–1920).**

he worked for three decades on a great many of the most important issues of the day for the postal system including the development of the telephone network. He combined public service with championing a wide number of causes, such as the preservation of commons and footpaths, the protection of ancient monuments and buildings, and local government in his adopted home of Haslemere in Surrey.

Hunter's death aged 69, just four months after his retirement in 1913, was a tragic loss to his devoted family. A century later we remember again the many achievements of this 'faithful servant of the people'.

Wicken Fen, Cambridgeshire, is the National Trust's oldest nature reserve; it came into their care from 1899.

Hunter's Family Origins

Robert Hunter was born in London in October 1844 and spent most of his life living or working there. But he was a Scot by ancestry, descending from a branch of the Hunters of Ayrshire, whose name is preserved in Hunterston Castle by the Firth of Clyde.

The fortunes of Robert Hunter's family owed much to the sea. His great uncle, Joseph Lachlan, founded a prestigious ship-broking firm that went on to serve as brokers to the Admiralty during the Crimean War.

Hunter's father, Robert Lachlan Hunter, left Ayrshire at a young age to go to sea, joining his brother aboard a ship. However, he disliked his captain and fled the ship's service, joining instead his uncle's company. (His brother died soon after, when the ship was lost at sea on her next voyage.)

Robert Lachlan Hunter next joined in a South Sea whaling expedition, and by the age of 24 he was Captain and part-owner of his own ship. His fortunes grew further, and in 1843 he married his cousin, Anne Lachlan. Their son, Robert, was born at the family home in Addington Square, Camberwell. The next year Robert Lachlan Hunter became a Master Mariner, but retired from the sea at the age of 40.

Captain Hunter continued to give his time to maritime business as the part owner of several ships, Deputy Chairman of the local marine board, and a member of Lloyds. He also promoted various charitable endeavours. He served as a special constable in Peel's Metropolitan Police force and was involved in the establishment in 1865 of the Belvedere Institute, now the Royal Alfred Seafarers' Society, to care for former seafarers and their families. In addition he served on the management committee of the Seaman's Hospital Society, which provided support for destitute seamen through the Dreadnought Hospital.

Such public-minded service clearly left a huge impression on young Robert, who displayed a similar dedication to charitable and public causes throughout his career.

Left: **Addington Square, Camberwell, where Robert Hunter was born in 1844.**

Childhood in South London

For the first two years of his life, Robert was a healthy child. But thereafter his health deteriorated, such that many thought he might become yet another casualty of the shockingly high rates of infant mortality that prevailed in London in the 1840s.

In an unpublished biography of her father, Hunter's daughter Dorothy wrote of these years that 'his slight, lithe frame and fair complexion gave him an appearance of great delicacy throughout his boyhood, but from the first his active little mind grew with uninterrupted vigour'. One elderly relative, being on the receiving end of young Robert's many questions, was said to have exclaimed: 'If that child goes on asking questions like that he will certainly die.'

Robert's family's close association with the sea gave him a love of playing with toy ships, acting out battles fought in the Crimean War. His father's sailors would return from trips abroad with exotic foods and even gifts of pet parrots. Robert remembered occasions such as his visit to the Great Exhibition of 1851 and the morning in 1852 when he was woken early to observe the funeral procession of the Duke of Wellington through the streets of central London.

From the age of six he attended a day school and then in 1853 the family moved to Denmark Hill. From here, Robert was sent to the local Grammar School, whose main building was designed by Sir Christopher Wren (Doctor Johnson was said to have completed his famous Dictionary in a summer house on the estate). Another famous resident of Denmark Hill was John Ruskin, who lived there from 1843 to 1872.

The extended Hunter family in south London enjoyed many gatherings and parties together, especially those involving singing and dances in the Scottish style. Robert remembered Christmases at his Uncle Joseph's and many other social events when 'glees, and part-songs, duets and trios were kept up till a late hour'. For their holidays the Hunters took trips to places like Hastings, Brighton, Teignmouth, Tunbridge Wells and Cromer. On a visit to North Wales with his aunt, Mrs Moncrief, Hunter first met Miss Emily Browning, the daughter of a family friend. The meeting was significant – she later became his first wife.

GRAND ENTRANCE TO THE GREAT EXHIBITION OF ALL NATIONS.

Top: The Grand Entrance to the Great Exhibition of 1851, which young Robert visited.

Above: The funeral procession of the Duke of Wellington in London, 1852, witnessed by 8-year-old Robert Hunter.

CHARTISM AND LAND REFORM

The Hunters belonged to the comfortable middle classes, but from time to time they were caught in the crossfire of moments of social unrest. The Chartist movement of the 1830s and 1840s was one of the earliest expressions of working-class political activism. The People's Charter of 1838 was a rallying point, and had six simple demands: universal male suffrage, following the limited reforms of 1832; payment for MPs, so that working men could be elected to Parliament; operation of the secret ballot, to ensure democratic freedom of expression; no property qualification for being an MP; equalizing of the population size of constituencies; and annual Parliaments.

Although many of these ideas are now accepted parts of the British political system, at the time they were seen as radical and even insurrectionary. The ruling class was greatly intimidated by the Chartists' demands and refused to even hear them discussed in Parliament. For many Chartists, the only option left was to strike or to make their demands heard through mass protests. Meetings and rallies were held throughout Britain but following a violent confrontation in Newport, Wales, in 1839, and strikes across England and Scotland in 1842, many of the Chartist leaders were arrested and imprisoned (and in some cases transported to Australia).

Another venture pursued by Chartist leader Feargus O'Connor was to set up cooperative land companies, later to become the National Land Company. From 1843 to 1848 several estates of land were purchased, in which workers held shares and which they managed collectively. Rosedene in Worcestershire was a Chartist cottage from this era, and is today looked after by the National Trust. Such radical approaches to questions of landownership were later to have influence on Hunter's own thinking.

One of the last great expressions of Chartism was the mass meeting held on Kennington Common in London in April 1848, at a time when revolutions were taking place across Europe. An estimated 150,000 people attended, and Robert's father served as one of the special constables recruited to deal with the potential threat. Robert later remembered his mother hurrying him back home, fearful of rumours that a great mob was about to rise up. Several of their neighbours in Camberwell were said to have been so nervous at the prospect of a Chartist uprising that they hid their valuables in water butts. In fact, the meeting dispersed peacefully.

Left: **Red-brick Rosedene cottage in Worcestershire, a Chartist cottage now looked after by the National Trust.**

Sprawling London

Denmark Hill is now in the middle of the sprawling south London suburbs. But when Hunter's family moved there in 1853 it was on the very edge of London. Green fields, still farmed, reached almost to the train station. Nevertheless, the pressure to build and develop was already very apparent, not least in the many fine houses and gardens that were being laid out.

As Hunter's daughter Dorothy later wrote, 'The rapid transformations which he witnessed of the surroundings of his early homes may well have fostered and encouraged his desire to secure for the dwellers in the town's gardens, parks or wide open spaces, as some reminder of the beauties and amenities of the country.'

Across London, north and south, fields and woods were giving way to bricks and mortar. The population of London from this time was growing at a staggering rate. Places like Wimbledon went from being a village of 4,500 people in 1851 to being inhabited by 55,000 people in 1911.

In 1861 the Hunters moved again, to Brixton. By the mid-1860s, the family made yet another move, this time to Carrick House in Surbiton, Surrey. This may have been a bid to escape the increasing urbanization of London life. At the time, Surbiton was still rural in character, little touched by the impact of trains and trams. The family were inspired to move there after a peaceful holiday staying near Hampton Court, where Robert and his sister enjoyed the sight of the deer in Bushey Park.

Below: **An aerial map of London, 1860.**

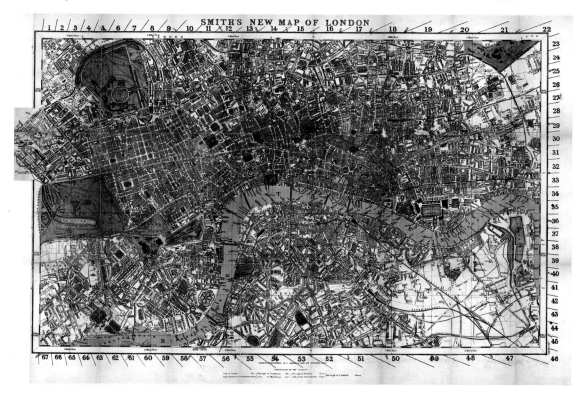

School and University

At Denmark Hill Grammar School, Robert's first-rate mind had been quickly recognized by the teachers and he was put into the highest ability sets. One fellow pupil later recalled that Robert and two other boys 'were ultimately so far advanced beyond those of the highest class in the school that a special class had to be created for their benefit'.

A great influence on Hunter's personal development at this time was Joshua Fitch (1824–1903), a distinguished educationalist. The pair took long walks together, during which they discussed 'manifold topics which press upon a young man's mind as he ceases to regard books from the point of view of a school boy and finds the world of life and letters opening before him'.

Hunter was especially struck by Fitch's commitment to public duty, quoting admirably his observation that there was 'no more animating thought for a young man entering life and conscious of power, than the reflection that he is not living for himself alone but that all his struggles after a higher life are distinct though humble contributions to the improvement of the race to which he belongs'.

At the age of 17 Robert matriculated at University College, London. Another influence here was the brilliant legal scholar Leonard Seeley (1831–93), who coached him for his examinations and helped to encourage the attention to detail and hard work that marked Robert's career.

Throughout his time as a university scholar, Robert excelled in his studies. In 1862 he gained an exhibition in English and won a commendation for his work on Political Economy. He attained his degree in 1865, with firsts in Logic and Moral Philosophy.

An accident left permanent damage in one eye, and Robert suffered bouts of ill-health throughout his life. Nevertheless, as a young man and student he enjoyed watching cricket at the Oval and rowing on the Thames and Cherwell. He was a member of the college rowing club, and later in life speculated as to

Left: **University College, London, where Robert Hunter excelled as a scholar.**

Below: **A portrait of Robert Hunter as a young man.**

Left: **The Yorkshire Moors, where Hunter enjoyed walking holidays.**

whether the time he spent on the water cost him his chance of winning the Gold Medal for scholarship in his year.

Robert was known to be warm-hearted and outgoing, and greatly relished social occasions and conversation. As a young man he enjoyed touring Scottish scenery with his family, and later took walking vacations to the Yorkshire Moors, the Cornish coast, northern France and the Swiss Alps. While at college he joined the Artists Rifle Corps, which had been established in 1860 as a volunteer unit for painters, architects, musicians and other professionals (Lord Leighton, George Frederic Watts and William Morris were all associated with the Artists Rifles). Like many moderate Englishmen of his generation, Hunter believed in incremental reform over more radical or revolutionary methods. Although the mid-19th century witnessed a spate of revolutions across Europe, Hunter was convinced that the rule of law was the best way to ensure moral and social cohesion. He was a loyal member of the Church of England and an instinctive Liberal in his politics.

Hunter had a strong faith in the power of human nature, in doing the 'right thing', and a disdain for dogmatism across both spiritual and temporal matters. Nevertheless, this did not diminish his ability to be critical of the accepted order. He became the president of his University's debating society and held debates on subjects such as the extension of the vote to women, a cause that he greatly supported.

In 1868 Hunter wrote to his fiancée to complain at the prevalence of Conservative opinion among the comfortable middle classes: 'It is a strange thing how much well-to-do merchants, Stockbrokers and lawyers set their faces against things that any one with the slightest belief in Justice, or the slightest discernment of the current of events must feel sure will come to pass sooner or later. Men wise in their own calling seem to be completely blind in matters of National importance.' He also admonished the Liberal MP for London University (Robert Lowe) for his arrogance and hubris: '... his prevailing fault is an over-weening self-confidence, and an inability to appreciate the good qualities of others.' These were qualities that Hunter strove hard to avoid, preferring instead to maintain good relations through diplomacy, manners and calmness under pressure.

Early Career

Robert Hunter considered a career in the Church, but chose the law instead. In spring 1866 he was articled to the firm Eyre and Lawson of Bedford Row.

Hunter soon found his new life to be a drudge. The work did not inspire him and the days were long and dull. He found diversion through further studying in the evenings and writing regular columns for the *Clapham Gazette*.

In the summer of 1866 he spotted an opportunity. The businessman (and later MP) Henry Peek offered prizes in return for original new essays on the topic of commons preservation. Peek was one of the leading commoners in Wimbledon, where the Common faced the threat of enclosure by the Lord of the Manor, Lord Spencer.

Hunter's chosen theme was 'The preservation of commons in the neighbourhood of the metropolis' and he dwelt at length on the public duties of landowners. They might have control over the soil, he argued, but this did not entitle them to deny wider public uses of the land. Rather, the role of a landlord was 'conferred in trust to be used for the benefit of the remainder of the community'.

Hunter argued for the extension of the Metropolitan Commons Act of 1866, which limited the enclosure of the remaining commons in London, to 'open spaces within the vicinity of all major towns and cities'. He also argued for the repeal of the Statute of Merton, the medieval law that was used by landlords to justify the enclosure of open lands without the consent of commoners.

Robert Hunter's essay did not win the competition. Nonetheless, it was recognized by the judges (who included politicians Cowper-Temple and Shaw-Lefevre) as being of exceptional quality. It was published in 1867 by Peek in an edition of six of the best essays from the competition.

Below: **Robert Hunter, the young lawyer.**

This boost to his confidence inspired Hunter in July 1867 to approach Philip Lawrence, solicitor to the Commons Preservation Society, to see if he could be taken into partnership. Lawrence invited him to dinner, but did not promise any more than the chance to be one of 20 articled clerks in his office.

Hunter was disappointed, but the chance to work directly on cases defending commons from unlawful enclosure was too tempting to resist. In August 1867 he took up a new role working for Lawrence at his offices at 6 Lincoln's Inn Fields.

The Battle for Common Land

T he Commons Preservation Society was one of the earliest environmental campaign groups in Britain. It first met in July 1865 at the Inner Temple chambers of the Liberal MP George Shaw-Lefevre and aimed to champion the cause of those commoners keen to resist the acts of landlords in enclosing open spaces. Their initial sphere of operation was greater London and their interests included commons and royal forests.

The immediate spark was the attempt by Lord Spencer to enclose Wimbledon Common in 1864, which had led to Parliamentary Select Committee investigation chaired by Frederick Doulton, Liberal MP for Lambeth. The Committee found that commons in London faced considerable pressure from enclosure and encroachment. The Metropolitan Commons Act of 1866 subsequently attempted to curtail such enclosures, but was insufficient to defend open spaces from the threat of extinction.

Commons were a unique form of open space. Unlike urban parks, which increasingly in the Victorian period were owned and managed as public assets by public authorities, commons were the private property of individual landlords. What made them distinct was the existence of certain rights over them, held by designated individuals or commoners. These included, for example, rights to graze animals, or to collect wood for timber or fuel, or to remove turfs. Rights of access were also sometimes allocated in this way. Commons otherwise were technically closed to public use even for walking, although in practice many people did claim rights of way by custom.

Below:
Wimbledon Common faced enclosure in Victorian times, but is now a Site of Special Scientific Interest (SSSI) and a Special Area of Conservation (SAC).

Left: Ludshott Common, acquired with the help of Hunter in 1908, is maintained by the National Trust.

The poorest agricultural land in a parish was often designated as common or waste and set aside for grazing animals while farmers tilled the open fields. The demise of the manorial courts, which regulated this collective way of farming, hastened the destruction of many commons. From the 16th century onwards they were often subject to enclosures, which during the 18th century were most often conducted through individual Acts of Parliament.

The 1845 General Enclosures Act put all future enclosures in the hands of a standing body of Enclosure Commissioners, and introduced some measure of protection for greens and commons. But this did not deter landlords, especially in urban areas, from seeking to use enclosure powers to turn commons into building plots. The prospect of the enclosure of places like Hampstead Heath, Wimbledon Common and Epping Forest brought the Commons Preservation Society to public attention.

At Wimbledon, Lord Spencer had proposed that a third of the Common should be enclosed and built over, while the remaining two thirds should be a public park for local people. Hunter commented in the *Clapham Gazette*: 'It was a little startling to some of the inhabitants of Wimbledon to be told suddenly that, as a great favour, they might be allowed to enjoy, under strict regulations, about two thirds of the Common which they had always supposed to be wholly theirs.'

Enclosure Struggles

Hunter worked on the Wimbledon case as a clerk for Philip Lawrence. In 1868 Lawrence was appointed as Solicitor to the Office of Works, and sold his business on to Hunter and two other senior partners, Tom Fawcett and Percy Horne. The firm of Fawcett, Horne and Hunter was subsequently appointed as solicitors to the Commons Preservation Society.

Hunter promised that he would 'make the Society more active than it has been of late'. In the process, he became the country's leading expert on the law of commons.

The Society's activism was sometimes direct. In his essay, Hunter had observed that 'any commoner whose rights are molested is clearly entitled to throw down the whole fencing or other obstruction erected'. He may have been thinking of the occasion in the 1840s when an enclosure was attempted on Wanstead Common by commoners who 'broke down the fence by the aid of a timber wagon which they christened Magna Carta, and marched in triumphant procession across the green'.

The tactic was used by the Commons Preservation Society in March 1866 when a team of 120 navvies was contracted to travel by train to Berkhamsted Common. Here they pulled down fences that had been put up by Earl Brownlow in order to enclose 430 acres (174ha) of open common land. After 1868 Hunter took over much of the work on the Berkhamsted case.

Hunter's method involved immersing himself in historical records, seeking out documents that often took him back to medieval times in order to prove the existence of legal rights of common. Manorial court rolls, leases and other estate papers were all closely examined.

Below:
Footpath from Berkhamsted Common to Berkhamsted. Hunter was involved in saving the Common from enclosure by Earl Brownlow of neighbouring Ashridge House.

This approach secured Hunter success in the Wimbledon case, when he was able to use an early 17th-century land transaction to prove that use rights extended across the whole of the Common.

Hunter used similar tactics in a sequence of cases heard throughout the 1860s and 1870s: Plumstead (1866–71), Hampstead (1868), Tooting Graveney (1868–71), Wandsworth (1870–71), Epping Forest (1865–71), Berkhamsted (1866–70), Ashdown Forest (1876–82), Dartford Heath (1874) and Banstead (1876).

Hunter drove himself and his colleagues to great extremes of effort in order to win cases. But time and again the evidence was sufficient to prevent a landlord from enclosing.

Below: **Epping Forest.**

EPPING FOREST

The Epping case, with which Hunter's name was closely associated, began in 1865, when Tom Willingale, his son and two nephews were sentenced to hard labour for selling firewood gathered from land around Hainault that had previously been fenced off by the owner, Reverend John Whittaker. When the Commons Preservation Society took up their case, they forced the Government into making a concession, although this amounted to an offer of little more than 600 acres (240ha) of land for increasing recreation, which was flatly refused by the Commons Preservation Society. Tom Willingale's death and the enclosure of more land in Wanstead led to increasing pressure on the Government, which announced an investigation by the Royal Commission.

Hunter discovered that the Corporation of the City of London had property interests in Wanstead and was therefore in possession of common rights over the forest. He persuaded the City to take up an action against the enclosures in 1871. By the time the case was heard in 1874, Hunter had collected considerable proof of the role of common rights in Epping Forest.

Evidence of cattle grazing and of the use of forest courts was deployed to demonstrate that Epping was indeed a common and should not face enclosure under the Metropolitan Commons legislation. The judge eventually found in Hunter's favour and awarded costs. The Royal Commission, when it reported a year later, came to similar conclusions.

Various Lords of the Manor of Epping, frustrated in their attempts to enclose and draw value from their estates, started to pass their rights over to the Corporation. By 1878 Epping was vested in the Corporation, who to this day retain responsibility for the extensive woods and open lands on the fringe of greater London. Loughton's Lopping Hall, erected as compensation to local people for the loss of their common rights, was constructed in 1879.

Family Life

Having established himself as a partner in the firm of Fawcett, Horne and Hunter in 1868, Robert Hunter was able finally to marry his fiancée, Emily Browning, at a service held in Oxford in March 1869. Tragically, she died in January 1872 during the course of a pregnancy.

He married again in 1877 to Ellen ('Nellie'), the daughter of Samuel Thomas Cann. By 1883 they had three daughters: Dorothy, Winifred and Margaret.

Also by 1883 the family had moved to a fine house, Meadfield, in Haslemere, Surrey. This was to be Hunter's home for the rest of his life and a place that he cherished beyond all. The area was greatly admired for its hilltop views and wide open spaces and was still largely untouched by industrialization or urbanization despite its proximity to the capital by train.

Many prominent writers and thinkers were to make homes in the area, including Alfred Lord Tennyson, Arthur Conan Doyle, George Bernard Shaw and Mrs Humphry Ward. It was a literary community of novelists and socially minded commentators.

With characteristic enthusiasm, Hunter leaped into local affairs, proposing a Haslemere committee for commons preservation in 1884 in order to prevent enclosures from despoiling the open look of the area. Conan Doyle, the creator of Sherlock Holmes, was later co-opted by Hunter onto the local committee for protecting Hindhead Commons.

Above: **Meadfield, Hunter's home in Haslemere.**

Below: **Lady Hunter, Robert Hunter's second wife.**

Benny Horne (family friend and solicitor to the National Trust), Sir Robert Hunter, his daughter Winnie and Canon Hardwicke Rawnsley in the Lake District, *c*.1900.

The General Post Office

Above: **The Penny Black: the world's first adhesive postage stamp.**

T he move to Haslemere coincided with another significant change in Hunter's life. In 1882 he was appointed as Solicitor to the General Post Office by Henry Fawcett MP, the Postmaster General in Gladstone's Liberal government.

We can detect in Hunter's work for the Post Office many of the same values and principles that he had demonstrated in his energetic defence of the commons. The Post Office of the time still reflected the radical influence of Rowland Hill. Hill had introduced the Penny Post in 1840 in order to make the postal service a universal provision that was accessible to all.

Hunter was to play a leading role in most of the innovations and developments that were to take place at the Post Office in the eventful years between 1882 and his retirement in 1913. In total he served 13 separate Postmasters General. He instituted the 'systematic examination' of all bills under consideration in Parliament in order to assess their impact on the Post Office's work.

He made his views known in 1888 at a time when the merits of introducing a new 'express' postal service were being debated. Hunter was reluctant to see a superior service introduced for a higher payment, since this offended the principle of uniformity, which 'was the principal merit of Sir Rowland Hill's reforms and which has obtained in reference to this service since 1840'.

Much of Hunter's work involved the careful legal operation of what was, in effect, a huge state monopoly. He prepared the 1893 Conveyance of Mails Act, which referred for settlement to the Railway and Canal Commission all

Left: **Victorian postal workers in a sorting office.**

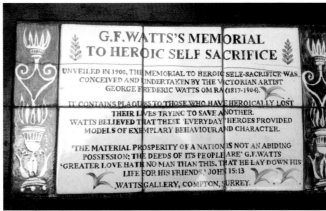

differences between the railway companies and the state as to remuneration for the carriage of mails. It saved the Post Office considerable amounts of money. He also enhanced the role and efficiency of the Post Office Savings Bank.

He brought to the Post Office the same painstaking attention to details that characterized his work on commons. It was said of his time at the Post Office that:

Left: **Postman's Park, London.**

Above: **Memorial in Postman's Park.**

> 'He made it his rule to form his own conclusions and to give his own advice instead of relying on opinions obtained from outside, and he believed that the Department profited by this policy in saving of time, in homogeneity and suitability of advice, and in the better training of his own assistants. The whole of the Post Office regulations … were drafted by Sir Robert Hunter, some of them two or three times to meet alterations.'

He was also a strong supporter of the work of the postmen themselves. Delivering the mail at this time was hard manual labour, and Hunter was a frequent advocate for better pay and conditions for Post Office workers. Postman's Park in the City of London was laid out from 1880 as a recreation ground for Post Office staff, and became the site of the painter George Frederic Watts' Memorial to Heroic Self Sacrifice, celebrating acts of heroism by ordinary people.

Below: **Henry Fawcett, seen here with his wife in a drawing by Ford Madox Brown, dated 1872.**

HENRY FAWCETT

Henry Fawcett (1833–84) was a Liberal MP who had been blinded in an accident early in his career. He was the brother of Tom, Hunter's legal partner, and was proud to have promoted Hunter to his role as Solicitor to the General Post Office. Fawcett had long admired Hunter's work for the Commons Preservation Society, having himself considered the land question as an influential Professor of Political Economy at Cambridge. He married Millicent Garrett, the campaigner for female suffrage.

The National Trust

On taking up his role with the Post Office, Hunter relinquished his role with the Commons Preservation Society. But he continued to campaign for commons and open spaces, and other causes. His ideas were formed through correspondence with the housing reformer Octavia Hill. For Hill, the provision of 'open air sitting rooms' for the poor through open green space was an essential complement to the provision of decent homes. Her failure to save Swiss Cottage Fields from development in 1875 was an unusual setback.

Hill's sister, Miranda, formed the Kyrle Society in the 1870s. The Kyrle campaigned to bring beauty to the lives of the poor. When an Open Spaces Sub-committee was established in 1879, Hunter became its honorary legal adviser and Chairman.

In the early 1880s Hill was involved in efforts to save the grounds of Sayes Court in Deptford, the historic home of the 17th-century writer John Evelyn. Evelyn's descendent wanted to give the garden to the nation, but Hunter pointed out to Hill that legally there was no straightforward way he could do so. Perhaps what was needed was a new form of legal vehicle, a land company that was able to hold assets on behalf of the wider public.

Hill wrote back to Hunter in August 1884 to express reservation that such a company could be established in time to save Sayes Court. She declined to share the idea with others, adding that 'unless our Company could be started much quicker than I think likely, or even perhaps possible … I almost feel as if it would be safer to go on with that plan which is started'. The prevarication did not bode well and Hill's efforts at Sayes Court were to no avail.

Undeterred, Hunter tried the idea out in other contexts. In 1884 he delivered an address to the annual congress of the National Association for the Promotion of Social Science. 'The central idea,' he said, 'is that of a Land Company formed … with a view to the protection of the public interests in the open spaces of the country.'

In February the following year Octavia Hill is said to have written to Hunter to suggest a name for 'the new company'. Hill's preference was for the name to include the word 'Trust', since 'people don't like unsuccessful business, but do like Charity where a little money goes a long way because of good commercial management'. Her suggestion was 'Commons and Garden Trust'. In a pencilled note at the top of the letter, Hunter wrote '?National Trust'.

Below: **The Kyrle Window in Octavia Hill's Birthplace House, Wisbech, Cambridgeshire. The Kyrle Society was founded by Octavia Hill and her sister; Octavia is pictured top left in the window.**

The idea of a National Trust lay dormant, or at least just below the surface, for the next seven or eight years. In 1889 we hear of Octavia Hill reporting to Hunter that George Shaw-Lefevre was not keen on the idea of a new company, correctly anticipating that it would steal a march on his own Commons Preservation Society. The idea of a land-holding organization gained more purchase across the Atlantic, where in 1891 the Trustees for Public Reservations in Massachusetts were established along the lines that Hunter had set out.

By 1893 fresh enthusiasm arose as a consequence of new threats to the Lake District. Canon Hardwicke Rawnsley had formed the Lake District Defence Society ten years earlier to protect against the encroachments of industry and railways. The availability of several properties for purchase led to further discussions, hosted by the Commons Preservation Society, on the formation and constitution of a landholding body 'to act as a corporation for the holding of lands of natural beauty and sites and houses of historic interest to be preserved intact for the nation's use and enjoyment'. Hunter prepared the objects of the body, and assembled names of those who might serve on its provisional council, including the Duke of Westminster.

The draft constitution of the new society was agreed at a meeting at Grosvenor House, the Duke's London residence, in July 1894. Formally, the National Trust for Places of Historic Interest and Natural Beauty came into existence as a legal company in 1895, 'on the express condition that it shall make no profit', with Hunter as its Chairman.

Above: **Octavia Hill led the campaign to save the grounds at Sayes Court.**

Below: **A copy of an early National Trust document: 'Its Aims and Its Work'. It includes the statement: 'It is thus the friend alike of historian, painter and poet.'**

The Trust's First Decade

As Chairman, Hunter played a highly influential role in the early years of the National Trust. He described the Trust as being 'the friend alike of historian, painter and poet'. For Hunter, it existed as an expression of 'patriotic interest' in those things which 'in the crush of our commercial enterprise and in the poverty of landholders or in the lack of local care, run risk of passing away'.

In those early years Hunter's vision of the Trust looked far beyond the few properties in its own care. He campaigned for places as diverse as Foyers waterfall at Loch Ness in Scotland, the Trinity Almshouses in Whitechapel and Churchyard Bottom Wood in Highgate, north London. In each of these cases Hunter pledged to bring the Trust's influence to bear, whether working alone or in partnership with 'kindred societies'.

The Trust began acquiring property straight away with the acquisition of Dinas Oleu in Barmouth, Wales, in its very first year. Typical of many of the places acquired by the Trust at this time it was a relatively small open space, a gorse-filled cliff-top where visitors could enjoy fresh air. It was donated by Fanny Talbot, an associate of John Ruskin. Barras Head in Cornwall, another cliff-top open space, followed soon after, as did a small piece of Wicken Fen in Cambridgeshire in 1899 (donated by Charles Rothschild).

Historic buildings also featured on the list of the Trust's earliest acquisitions. Alerted by the Society for the Protection of Ancient Buildings (SPAB), the Trust acquired Alfriston Clergy House in Sussex in 1896 for a nominal £10 and rescued it from dereliction. Hunter personally negotiated the acquisition of Kanturk Castle in County Cork in 1900, while Tintagel Post Office was acquired for £200 in 1903.

Left: **Dinas Oleu in Wales was the first National Trust property, acquired in March 1895.**

This interest in buildings is likely to have come from Hunter himself and from the Trust's close association with the SPAB. But the experience of acquiring Barrington Court in Somerset in 1907 was relatively unusual at this time: country houses did not feature heavily among the interests of the Trust's founders. Barrington itself was later to prove a burden on the Trust, and was an early lesson in the need to ensure financial prudence.

Instead, the first decades of the National Trust were marked more by its campaigns for open landscapes. The Trust was most active in those areas in which its founders had direct influence. In the Lake District, Rawnsley took to the streets in order to raise the funds to acquire Brandelhow in 1902 and the Gowbarrow estate in 1906. Octavia Hill was influential in ensuring the acquisition of hilltops near her home in Kent: Toys Hill, Ide Hill and Mariners Hill.

Hunter promoted the purchase of Hindhead Commons and the Devil's Punch Bowl in Surrey in 1906 following a fundraising appeal. This was a significant acquisition of 750 acres (300ha) of land, from the estate of Whitaker Wright, a local financier who had committed suicide rather than face jail for fraud.

Nutcombe Down in Surrey and Bramshott Chase in Hampshire followed in 1908, gifts of the philanthropist Marion James. Ludshott Common in Hampshire was acquired following a campaign led by James, while Marley Common, West Sussex, was bought from the Leconfield Estate in 1911. Blakeney Point in Norfolk, meanwhile, was acquired in 1912.

By 1908 the Trust had 30 separate properties, which had more than doubled by 1914 at which time it held just short of 6,000 acres (2,400ha) of land. The Trust was still small, but perhaps the most significant development in these years took place in 1907 when the charity acquired its own Act of Parliament.

The Act was undoubtedly Hunter's most pivotal achievement as first Chairman of the Trust, demonstrating his far-sighted vision and establishing a firm foundation for the future.

Left: **Barras Head, near Tintagel, Cornwall.**

Above: **The 14th-century Alfriston Clergy House in Sussex was the first building to come under the care of the National Trust.**

'FOR THE BENEFIT OF THE NATION'

The National Trust Act of 1907 described the charity's purpose as being to promote the 'permanent preservation for the benefit of the nation of lands and ... buildings of beauty or historic interest'. The Act gave the Trust its unique power to hold land inalienably. The trustees, having declared property inalienable, were prevented from ever disposing of such land without the explicit consent of Parliament. It is from this that the Trust derives its mission to look after special places 'for ever, for everyone'.

Protecting Buildings and Monuments

Until 1882, no legal protection existed for monuments in England, although many were under threat from demolition, degradation or over-zealous 'restoration'. Concern for the plight of historic buildings led William Morris to establish the Society for the Protection of Ancient Buildings in 1877, today the country's longest-running heritage charity.

In 1882 the Ancient Monuments Act finally passed into law, thanks to the efforts of Liberal MP Sir John Lubbock (later Lord Avebury). It was the first piece of legislation to offer protection for the most important archaeological sites in the country, although its powers were weak.

Hunter was active in supporting the work that went into the 1882 Act and subsequent Acts. His legal knowledge was unrivalled and greatly valued. He was asked by Lord Avebury to prepare a particular clause of the 1900 Ancient Monuments Act because this was deemed better than having 'the drafting … entrusted to the Office of Works'.

Hunter was a great influence on the 1913 Ancient Monuments Act, drafting an early version of the legislation which led to the establishment of an Advisory Board and enhanced powers for monument protection. Hunter also secured changes to Lloyd George's budgets of 1909 and 1910 in order to empower the Inland Revenue to accept land and buildings in place of cash payment for meeting death duties. 'Acceptance in lieu' is now an accepted means by which assets are secured for the nation by the National Trust and other heritage bodies.

Below:
Stonehenge, near Amesbury in Wiltshire.

STONEHENGE

Stonehenge was one of the monuments protected under the 1882 Act, but its management remained a long-running issue. At this time the stone circle remained in private hands. Around 1900 it was fenced in to protect it from damage. For Hunter this epitomized the conflict between access and preservation.

He said: 'Those who would surround Stonehenge with barbed wire, and filter the nation through a toll-gate, are the men who cannot rise from details and measurements to the conception of a monument as a whole; men who, in another connection, would delight to pick a flower to pieces and explain its parts, but could not appreciate its beauty of form and colour when alive. The work of such antiquaries is most valuable; but there is no life in it.'

Campaigning for Special Places

Hunter continued to campaign for special places of all kinds, even while he served in a prominent public position at the General Post Office. He was involved in efforts for places as diverse as the Admiralty Buildings in Whitehall, St Cross Hospital in Winchester, Lincoln's Inn Fields in Holborn, the banks of the river Avon, the Geffrye Almshouses in Shoreditch (now the Geffrye Museum), and Leighton House, Kensington – formerly the studio-home of Victorian artist Frederic, Lord Leighton, and now the Leighton House Museum.

Hunter had a particular interest in London's architecture and planning. He served for a brief period on the managing committee of the New Hospital for Women, but resigned after the hospital was given permission by the Board of Works to build within 20 feet (6m) of Euston Road. Hunter had urged the Committee 'not to break the present line of building, on account of the ill-effect which would follow from encroaching upon the air-space', and never forgave them for the decision.

He devoted much time to opposing the extension of the underground network to Hampstead Heath from 1903 to 1908. He described this project as 'more difficult, long-drawn-out, and discouraging than any other scheme of a similar nature'.

Above: **Detail from Leighton House Museum. The collections here include paintings and sculptures by Leighton and his contemporaries.**

Later Hunter was a key figure on the board of the Hampstead Garden Suburb Trust, founded by the social reformer Henrietta Barnett in 1906 (herself an early follower of Octavia Hill). The laying out of new houses and gardens in this part of north London was based on principles that Ebenezer Howard had first set out and which had been put into effect at Letchworth Garden City: mixed, low-density housing, set on tree-lined avenues, with plenty of space for gardens separated by neat hedges.

Hunter also served as the first president of the Federation of Rambling Clubs from 1905, a grouping that was a forerunner of today's Ramblers Association.

Left: **The Geffrye Museum. The collections here show how homes and gardens have been used over the past 400 years, reflecting the changes in society and style.**

Haslemere and Hindhead

ack home in Haslemere, Hunter served as the first Chairman of the Parish Council, which was formed following the Local Government Act of 1894. The Council oversaw the workings of the Poor Law system, and of the Highways Board. He was evidently a great success at this, too. The *Surrey Times* in 1896 reported:

Left: **Sir Robert Hunter (far left)** in 1913. The occasion was the acceptance of deeds for Reigate Hill, part of which was given to the Borough of Reigate, Surrey. Reigate Hill is now a Site of Special Scientific Interest (SSSI) in the care of the National Trust.

'No parish council in the county has done better work than the Haslemere council. Sanitation, allotments, charities, lighting, roads, footpaths and waste lands have been thoroughly but prudently looked after, and the burden thrown upon the rate-payer in the shape of a rate for Parish Council purposes has been limited to ½d in the pound. A better combination of efficiency with economy could not be wished for, or hoped for. The result is due to the spirit in which the members of a thoroughly representative council have worked together and, above all, to the invaluable help accorded by Sir Robert Hunter as Chairman.'

Hunter later attempted to block plans to enlarge the parish church at Haslemere, which he felt 'would destroy its character and harmony with the quiet village surroundings'.

Left: St Bartholomew's Church in Haslemere.

HINDHEAD COMMONS

The village of Hindhead is perhaps best known for its Commons. Hunter would no doubt have been proud to see the abundant wildlife at this designated Area of Outstanding Natural Beauty (AONB), with views across the Devil's Punch Bowl. A project lasting 20 years came to its conclusion in 2011 when a new tunnel bypass here was completed, replacing the old A3 road – a notorious bottleneck in its day. The land is already reverting 'back to nature' as a result.

The old A3 now enjoyed by walkers at the Devil's Punch Bowl, Hindhead Commons – 'the gateway to the Surrey hills'.

Retirement and Final Days

Hunter was knighted in 1894, and subsequently elevated to CB in 1909 and KCB 1911. These honours were recognition of his many achievements during a long and hardworking career. They also reflected his close alliance to the Liberal establishment.

The nationalization of the telephone service was one of the last major projects Hunter undertook in his role at the Post Office. It consumed a great deal of his time and energy. Indeed, the effort of the case may well have hastened Hunter's death, in the same year that he retired (1913).

When telephones were first introduced from 1878 they were provided by private companies such as the National Telephone Company. The Post Office assumed increasing control and under the terms of the 1909 Telegraph Arbitration Act became the monopoly supplier of the telephone service.

Hunter's role was to negotiate the compensation settlement with the National Telephone Company. Following 72 days of arbitration, Hunter reduced the bill from £21 million to £12½ million.

By this time Hunter was the second highest-paid official working for the Post Office. Having concluded the deal with the National Telephone Company, he retired his position in July 1913. His death from toxaemia just four months later on 6 November 1913 was a cruel end, depriving him of a long and healthy retirement in his beloved Surrey hills.

Below: **Telegraph poles reflected in a river. Not everyone welcomed this addition to the landscape.**

POLES AND PYLONS IN THE LANDSCAPE

The spread of telecommunications, from telegraph wires to the new methods of telephony, was to leave a lasting impact on the landscape. Not everyone welcomed the intrusion. In his position as Chair of the Hindhead Commons Committee, Hunter agreed in 1907 to 'request the National Trust to take any action they might think fit to prevent the disfigurement of the Commons by poles'. Effectively he was lobbying himself (since he was also Chair of the National Trust) about a problem caused as a result of his own professional work for the Post Office! Later, in 1912, Hunter was to observe jokingly that his work for the open spaces movement was 'some compensation from the point of view of the public, to the work he, as solicitor, does for the P.O. in forcing unwilling communities to accept overhead wires'.

Sir Robert Hunter's Legacy

Hunter's funeral was held in the parish church at Haslemere on 10 November 1913. Many notable public figures were in attendance, along with many 'men and women from all ranks' from his department of the Post Office.

The day before Hunter's death, the National Trust announced the acquisition of Box Hill in Surrey. Places like this, not least the commons in the vicinity of Haslemere itself, today provide Hunter's most visible and enduring legacy. The woods and water of Waggoners Wells were purchased by public subscription in 1919 in memory of the Trust's first Chairman.

Numerous people noted the loss of Hunter from their lives. Social reformer Samuel Barnett observed that Hunter 'combined in a rare degree a deep love of beauty, legal acumen, and unfathomed patience'. He added that Hunter was not 'an effective speaker, and therefore the world did not know what it owed him'.

A correspondent of Hunter's, in the final year of his life, praised him for his ability to 'break down adhesions or reduce the friction in Governmental and Corporation machinery'. Meanwhile in *The Spectator* his life's work was praised as 'one long record of services of which it would be difficult to exaggerate the value … He laid the whole country … under a debt which few of the present generation realize.'

Hunter's daughter Dorothy wrote of 'his unfailing gentleness and chivalry in all personal relationships; his loyalty in friendship; his unselfishness in giving credit to others; his deep love of beauty in all its forms, together with a happy readiness to enjoy the pleasant and amusing little things that sweeten daily life; and withal his quiet, level-headed idealism, founded on a steadfast belief in the power of goodness and the progress of humanity'.

Below: **Memorial stone to Sir Robert Hunter at Waggoners Wells, near Grayshott on the Hampshire/Surrey border.**

IN MEMORY OF SIR ROBERT HUNTER

Who laboured in the restless City's roar
And gave his strength to service of the State
With Nature did his soul communicate
And loving her – he loved the people more.
Unresting ever, armed with wisdom's lore,
True knight, he stood to guard the open gate
Kept paths and common still inviolate
To bless the nation with their restful store.
Now has he gone to where the world is fair
And free for all, and we who weep and mourn
The wise, great hearted, gentle, genial man,
May hear his voice call clear from yonder bourne
All selfish ways and worldliness to ban
And all earth's common loveliness to share.

Sonnet by Hardwicke Rawnsley

Dorothy shared much of her father's passion and commitment to public service. She stood (unsuccessfully) for Parliament in 1907 and served for many years (to 1966) on the National Trust's Council.

It is necessary to redress the balance given by some accounts of the early years of the National Trust, in which Hunter is still occasionally referred to as a 'somewhat shadowy' figure who acts as handmaiden to the far greater achievements of personalities like Octavia Hill and Hardwicke Rawnsley.

In truth, Hunter was the principal force in the legal creation of the National Trust. The Trust emerged from a nexus of ideas and thoughts among like-minded people in the late 1870s and early 1880s, which gained political purchase through Gladstone's Liberal administration. The trio of Hill, Hunter and Rawnsley are rightly recognized as the Trust's founders, but the network of influence from which it emerged could be extended to include Henry Fawcett, James Bryce, Baron Eversley and a host of others.

The trio was an equal and mutually dependent partnership, but attempts were made to impress different versions of their history immediately after their deaths. Rawnsley used an obituary of Hunter to claim for himself the inspiration of the idea of the National Trust, a cause in which Hunter was merely 'the first person consulted'. Meanwhile Donald Mathieson, Secretary to the National Trust at the time of the organization's 50th anniversary, promoted the thought that 'it was Octavia Hill who boldly proposed that the new body should be called The National Trust'.

Hunter was more likely to have been the inspiration for the name and indeed idea of the National Trust. Even if he was not, however, Hunter's role was still pivotal. He gave the Trust its legal definition, served as its first Chairman and fought many of its early battles to save special places for future generations. Far from being a shadowy figure, he was recognized publicly at the time as being the Trust's main leader and figurehead. He deserves to be better remembered to posterity for this and the many other achievements of his long and successful career.

Left: **Box Hill, Surrey**, part of the North Downs and in the care of the National Trust.

Above: Waggoners Wells, a series of ponds linked by streams and waterfalls.

Below: Memorial plaque to Sir Robert in Haslemere Church.

TO THE HONOURED MEMORY OF
ROBERT HUNTER M.A.. K.C.B.
27TH OCT. 1844   6TH NOV. 1913
(SOLICITOR TO THE GENERAL POST OFFICE 1881-1913)
A TIRELESS WORKER IN THE CAUSE OF PRESERVING
AND ACQUIRING OPEN SPACES FOR THE FREE
ENJOYMENT OF THE PUBLIC IN TOWN AND COUNTRY
A FOUNDER AND FIRST CHAIRMAN
OF THE NATIONAL TRUST
A REGULAR WORSHIPPER IN THIS CHURCH DURING
HIS 32 YEARS RESIDENCE AT MEADFIELD
ALSO HIS WIFE ELLEN 10TH SEPT. 1851 · 25TH JAN. 1932
WHOSE LOVE BEAUTY AND WIT WERE HIS SUPPORT AND DELIGHT
ERECTED IN GRATITUDE AND AFFECTION BY THEIR THREE DAUGHTERS

Places to Visit

There are many places of beauty and interest for which as a nation we are indebted to Robert Hunter and his fellow co-founders of the National Trust; listed here are just a few of them. Contact them or visit their websites for further information, including details of opening dates and times where applicable.

Hindhead Commons and the Devil's Punch Bowl

London Road, Hindhead, Surrey GU26 6AB
01428 681050
Email hindhead@nationaltrust.org.uk
www.nationaltrust.org.uk/hindhead-and-devils-punchbowl/
With the opening of the A3 tunnel, this landscape has been returned to its former tranquillity and beauty.

Ludshott Common and Waggoners Wells

Grayshott, Hampshire GU26 6DT
01428 751338
Email info@ntludshott.org.uk
www.ntludshott.org.uk/
From the higher parts of the common, panoramic views over east Hampshire to the South Downs can be enjoyed. Hunter was involved in the acquisition of Ludshott Common in 1908, and Waggoners Wells was purchased in 1919 in his memory.

Blakeney Point National Nature Reserve

Morston Quay, Morston, Norfolk NR25 7BH
01263 740241
Email blakeneypoint@nationaltrust.org.uk
www.nationaltrust.org.uk/blakeney
This sand and shingle spit, with its salt marsh and uninterrupted views of the coastline, is a paradise for all kinds of wildlife.

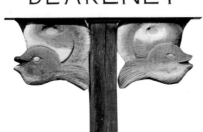

Right: **The coastal village of Blakeney in Norfolk; with the help of Sir Robert Hunter, Blakeney Point was acquired by the National Trust in 1912.**

Alfriston Clergy House

The Tye, Polegate, East Sussex BN26 5TL
01323 871961
Email alfriston@nationaltrust.org.uk
www.nationaltrust.org.uk/alfriston-clergy-house/
A rare 14th-century Wealden 'hall house', which was the first building to be acquired by the National Trust, in 1896.

Wicken Fen National Nature Reserve

Lode Lane, Wicken, Cambridgeshire CB7 5XP
01353 720274
Email wickenfen@nationaltrust.org.uk
www.nationaltrust.org.uk/wicken-fen/
Wicken Fen is one of Europe's most important wetlands. Part of it first came to the Trust in 1899, and further gifts and bequests have enabled new areas to be opened for public access.

Epping Forest

High Beach Visitor Centre, High Beach, Essex IG10 4AE
020 8508 0028
Email epping.forest@cityoflondon.gov.uk
www.cityoflondon.gov.uk/things-to-do/green-spaces/epping-forest
Epping Forest is London's largest open space, stretching from Manor Park in east London to just north of Epping in Essex.

Octavia Hill's Birthplace House

8 South Brink, Wisbech, Cambridgeshire PE13 1JB
01945 476358
Email info@octaviahill.org
www.octaviahill.org
This museum is dedicated to the life and work of Octavia Hill, and contains much of relevance to the founding of the National Trust and its work in the earliest years.